# Michael Jordan

JUNIOR ■ WORLD ■ BIOGRAPHIES

A JUNIOR *BLACK AMERICANS OF ACHIEVEMENT* BOOK

# Michael Jordan

## SEAN DOLAN

CHELSEA JUNIORS

a division of CHELSEA HOUSE PUBLISHERS

*English-language words that are italicized in the text can be found in the glossary at the back of the book.*

**Chelsea House Publishers**

EDITORIAL DIRECTOR  Richard Rennert
EXECUTIVE MANAGING EDITOR  Karyn Gullen Browne
COPY CHIEF  Robin James
PICTURE EDITOR  Adrian G. Allen
CREATIVE DIRECTOR  Robert Mitchell
ART DIRECTOR  Joan Ferrigno
PRODUCTION MANAGER  Sallye Scott

**JUNIOR WORLD BIOGRAPHIES**

SENIOR EDITOR  Martin Schwabacher
SERIES DESIGN  Marjorie Zaum

**Staff for MICHAEL JORDAN**

EDITORIAL ASSISTANT  Erin McKenna
PICTURE RESEARCHER  Sandy Jones
COVER ILLUSTRATION  Bradford Brown

First Printing

1  3  5  7  9  8  6  4  2

Library of Congress Cataloging-in-Publication Data

Dolan, Sean.
  Michael Jordan / Sean Dolan.
    p. cm.—(Junior world biographies)
  Includes bibliographical references and index.
Summary: Examines the life and basketball career of the high-scoring player with the Chicago Bulls, who made a brief attempt to play minor league baseball in 1994.
ISBN 0-7910-2394-X
    0-7910-2395-8 (pbk.)
  1. Jordan, Michael, 1963– —Juvenile literature. 2. Basketball players—United States—Biography—Juvenile literature. [1. Jordan, Michael, 1963– . 2. Basketball players. 3. Afro-Americans—Biography.] I. Title. II. Series.
GV884.J67D65  1996                                    95-22972
796.323'092—dc20                                          CIP
                                                           AC

# Contents

*Michael Jordan soars for a layup over Reggie Miller and Mark Jackson of the Indiana Pacers in his first game back from retirement. His uniform number, 45, was a brief carryover from his baseball career.*

# CHAPTER

# 1

# The Brightest Light on Broadway

On his eagerly awaited comeback tour, the star had played four out-of-town previews before bringing his show to the Big Apple. In Indianapolis, in Boston, in his hometown of Chicago, and in Atlanta, the reviews had been mixed. The critics had not been unkind, but still there was a sense of disappointment. Yes, there had been moments of brilliance, but no true sustained excitement, and a certain element of drama had been missing from the star's performance.

But all that was sure to change in New York City, everyone believed. The star loved the spotlight, and there was no brighter spotlight than New York, the media capital of the country. If the star had not yet truly dazzled, it must have been because he was waiting to play on Broadway.

Such was the hope of the 19,763 fans who filed into a sold-out Madison Square Garden on Tuesday night, March 28, 1995. Some of them had paid as much as $1,500 for the privilege of attending that night's performance. It was a demanding audience with extremely high expectations, one that would not be easily overwhelmed. Priding itself on its sophistication, it would be satisfied with nothing less than the extraordinary.

"If I can make it there, I'll make it anywhere" go the lyrics of an extremely popular song about New York, and that sentiment was generally considered true. There was simply no tougher audience to impress, particularly when the scheduled performance was a basketball game. New Yorkers prided themselves on their knowledge of "hoops." "The city game," they called it.

The star these fans had paid such a high price to see was Michael Jordan, the recently returned shooting guard of the Chicago Bulls of the National Basketball Association (NBA). Just 17 months earlier, Jordan had stood at the absolute top of his profession. He had compiled a record of individual achievement unmatched in the game's history: three straight NBA titles; seven straight scoring championships; three Most Valuable Player (MVP) awards; a *Rookie* of the Year Award; one national college-basketball championship; two Olympic gold medals; the highest per-game scoring average in the NBA's history for the regular season, playoffs, and All-Star game; nine straight years as an All-Star; seven straight years as an All-NBA first-team selection; and he was the only player in history to win a scoring championship and be honored as the league's best defensive player in the same season.

And *what* he had done on a basketball court spoke even less about his game than *how* he had done it. His nickname, Air, said almost all one needed to know about the way he played, for it was in the air that the six-foot-six-inch Jordan seemed to spend most of his time during the 48 minutes of an NBA game. Jordan was the most gracefully spectacular player in the league, its highest jumper, most thrilling dunker, and owner of the most indefensible collection of moves. "Trying to describe the way Michael Jordan plays is like trying to describe a beautiful piece of music," wrote longtime NBA observer P. C. Munson. "You can't. You have to listen to the one, and you have to see the other."

For very good reason, most of those who had paid close attention to Jordan's career believed that he was the best player ever to play the game. Bobby Knight, the notoriously critical coach of Indiana University, went one step further. Not only was Jordan the best ever to *have* played the game, said Knight; he "is the best that ever *will* play the game."

Then, at the young age of 30, after just nine seasons in the league, having just led Chicago to its third straight NBA championship, Jordan walked away. Mentally exhausted and greatly saddened by the murder of his beloved father, Jordan shocked everyone by announcing his retirement just before the 1993–94 NBA season.

While he amused himself finding out whether his athletic skills would enable him to enjoy a second career as a professional baseball player, the Bulls suffered. They were knocked out of the playoffs early, in the second round, in 1994. The following season was even worse. Chicago struggled all season just to win as many games as they lost, and there seemed little reason to hope that they would do much better in the playoffs.

And then the savior returned. The official announcement of his comeback was beautifully terse. "I'm back," was all the press release said, but in basketball circles those two words were enough. Stocks in the multitude of companies for which Jordan did commercial endorsements soared with the announcement. Opponents seemed almost to tremble at the news. Larry Brown, coach of the Indiana Pacers, seemed to concede defeat to Chicago even though his team was many games ahead of the Bulls in the standings. "With Jordan they'll win the championship again," he said. "Definitely."

But a funny thing happened. At first, the savior seemed human; the game's most superhuman player fell to earth. He looked rusty and hesitant, somewhat unsure of himself, and his jump shot was off. Better than a 50 percent shooter throughout his career, he made less than 40 percent of his shots—a horrendous mark—in the first four games of his return. Even more telling, he appeared more willing than ever before to settle for his jump shot and less able to bewilder defenders with his slithering, serpentine drives to the basket, in which he seemed to fake or feint or change direction a dozen times or more in covering just 15 feet of hardwood.

There was no doubt that he was still a superb player; he just did not seem to be the real Michael Jordan yet. Even worse, Chicago did not seem to perform any better with him. They won just two of his first four games back.

But, most observers agreed, the real test would come in New York. The New York Knicks were the Bulls' fiercest rivals, their toughest competition during the championship years and their successors as the Eastern Conference's best team during Jordan's first season away. Jordan especially disliked the Knicks, both for their very physical style of play and their habit of "talking trash" to opponents. The one New York player Jordan seemed to dislike most was John Starks, the unfortunate Knick who was usually assigned to guard him.

From the game's opening *tip-off*, there was no doubt that the real Jordan was back, ready to play, and possibly better than ever. He hit the

*Michael Jordan had asserted his dominance over John Starks many times in the past, but his fans wondered if he could rise to the occasion again after a two-year layoff.*

game's first basket, a vintage jump shot from the left wing. He scored his team's next basket, a jump shot from the top of the key. He missed his third shot but then hit four more in a row, including a soaring baseline drive. When the first quarter ended, he had already scored 20 points, and Starks looked *shell-shocked*. Jordan wound up the first half—"one of the most preposterous first halves in the history of [Madison Square] Garden," wrote sportswriter Ira Berkow—with 35 points.

The game was as much a classic as Jordan's performance. After trailing most of the way, Chicago caught New York early in the *fourth quarter* and raced ahead to a nine-point lead. But the Knicks clawed their way back, until with just under 30 seconds to play the score was tied at 109. Isolated with the ball against Starks at the top of the key, Jordan feinted right, then left, then right again, before launching himself to the left with a hard crossover dribble. Scrambling desperately to catch up, Starks somehow succeeded in cutting off his path, whereupon Jordan planted his left foot, crossed his dribble over to the right, and drove hard in that direction.

Again Starks rushed to recover, scuttling frantically after him. Just right of the foul line,

Jordan planted his right foot this time and, driving off it, rose into the air. Hurrying behind him, hopelessly earthbound at this point, Starks scurried by the place where Jordan had just been. "There was nothing left for Starks to guard," wrote sportswriter Mike Wise, "nothing more than a living legend."

More than three feet of air now flowed between the bottom of Jordan's sneakers and that small place on the court from where he had lifted off. At the height of his jump the ball was balanced perfectly in the fingers of his right hand, steadied by his left, both arms extended above and slightly out in front of his head. With infinite grace, he released his shot. The ball swished through the net, coming down as softly as Jordan himself had returned to the Garden court a fraction of a second earlier. The basket constituted his 54th and 55th points of the night.

Yet the Knicks would not be *vanquished*. With 14 seconds remaining, Starks made two *foul shots* to again tie the score. As Jordan sped the length of the court with the ball, racing the clock and the Knicks, a dizzying array of spins and jukes once more left Starks lagging behind as he flew into the lane. This time, however, Starks got help, as his giant teammates Patrick Ewing and Charles Oakley rushed to his aid. At the height of his jump, Jordan was confronted by the seven-foot Ewing.

It seemed that Jordan had no choice but to throw up a hopeless shot, but at the very last instant he spotted his teammate Bill Wennington standing unguarded beneath the basket. If it took three men to try to stop Jordan, one of the other Bulls had to be free, and that man was Wennington. Jordan's perfect pass hit the sometimes clumsy Chicago center right in the hands, and with three seconds to go Wennington dunked the game-winning basket.

"I'm starting to get a little hang of it again," Jordan told reporters in the jubilant Chicago locker room after the game. He had just scored the

*Michael Jordan flies past John Starks during his triumphant return to Madison Square Garden on March 28, 1995. Jordan scored 55 points during the contest, silencing doubters who wondered if he had lost a step since his retirement.*

most points in a single game in the history of Madison Square Garden, but the true significance of his performance was far greater than that. "Some players simply transcend the game and everything around them, and he's one of them," said the Knicks coach, Pat Riley. "That's the fun of it," Jordan explained. "Tomorrow you don't know what I might do."

"He reminds us of something," said the commissioner of the NBA, David Stern, who was on hand to witness the historic occasion. "He reminds us how we want our sports to be. He expands the possibilities."

Still, it was a 10-year-old admirer who was interviewed by sportswriter Mike Lupica at "the Cage," the famous basketball court at West Fourth Street in New York City's Greenwich Village, who said it best about Jordan's epic performance. In their own way, the boy's words echoed Bobby Knight's appraisal. "Michael's the man," the boy said. "Michael's the man until he dies."

*At age 12, Jordan's fierce concentration and competitive-ness were already evident, though his favorite sport at the time was baseball, not basketball.*

# 2

# Willful and Lazy

Michael Jeffrey Jordan was born on February 17, 1963, to James and Deloris Jordan. James Ronald Jordan was their oldest child; he was followed by Deloris, Larry, and then Michael, who was himself followed several years later by Roslyn.

Both of Michael's parents were from small towns in North Carolina. Michael was born in Brooklyn, New York, where his father was attending school as part of his job training at General Electric. James Jordan worked first as a forklift operator and then as a dispatcher for General Electric in Wallace, North Carolina.

Michael was born with a nosebleed, and the doctors worried that this was a sign that something more serious was wrong. They kept the baby in the hospital for several days after his mother was sent home, but he proved to be in good health, even though he would have nosebleeds for no apparent reason until he was five years old.

Michael's parents would often have reason to worry about him, for as a young boy he had a mischievous, daredevil streak. As a two-year-old, he was almost electrocuted in a backyard accident, and at age five he nearly cut off his big toe while playing with an ax.

Disciplining Michael was often useless. Outgoing and charming, he was also extremely strong willed. "If there was something to be tried," his mother remembers, "he was the one to try it."

When Michael was seven, his family moved to Wilmington, a small city by the Atlantic Ocean in southeast North Carolina. It was in Wilmington that Michael learned to play basketball. According to his father, "every kid in the neighborhood" would come to the Jordan house because it was the only one with a basketball court.

Most of these schoolboy hoopsters were friends of Michael's older brothers and were between the ages of 10 and 18. As the youngest and smallest player, Michael had to learn quickly and play hard if he wanted to take part in the games.

Michael's main competition in those backyard games was his brother Larry, who was one year older and a great leaper. For many years, Larry invariably won their hard-fought one-on-one contests, which often ended with punches being thrown.

But for a long time, basketball was not even Michael's favorite sport. Baseball was, and it was as a baseball player that he first attracted attention for his athletic abilities.

"The way he played baseball in Little League, he made me become a fan," his father once remembered. "If I wouldn't take him to play ball, he'd look so pitiful, like he'd lost every friend in the world and was all by himself. You'd take one look at him and say, 'Okay, let's go.'"

To this day, Michael considers the state baseball championship he won with his Babe Ruth League team to be one of his greatest achievements. "My favorite memory, my greatest accomplishment," he said in 1991, "was when I got the Most Valuable Player award when my team won the state baseball championship. That was the first thing I accomplished in my life, and you always remember the first. I remember I batted over .500, hit five home runs in seven games, and pitched a one-hitter to get us into the championship game."

Although Michael's athletic abilities thrilled his father, other aspects of his personality did not. James Jordan had grown up poor, and he believed in hard work. But Michael, he said, "was probably the laziest kid I had. He would give every last dime of his allowance to his brothers and sisters and kids in the neighborhood to do his chores for him. . . . That really got me." To James

Jordan, who was already working in the tobacco fields on a tractor at age 10, his son's attitude toward work was difficult to accept.

But Michael's attitude toward hard work changed in his sophomore year at Elmsley A. Laney High School in Wilmington. By now, basketball had replaced baseball as Michael's favorite sport. He fully expected to make the varsity basketball team, but Coach Fred Lynch cut him from the squad.

*Jordan remembers feeling "goony looking" in high school, and he was called Bald Head by some of his classmates.*

*After being cut from his high school team as a sophomore, Jordan worked furiously to improve his game, rising at 6:00 A.M. so he could practice before school. The next year, he became the star of the varsity team.*

The event shocked him. "I'll never forget how hurt I was," he said years later. "I cried." He was so angry that he could not even bring himself to root for the varsity team to win.

He responded by working on his game. Determined to prove the coach wrong, he rose each morning at six o'clock to practice by himself before school began. He kept this up for the rest of his time in high school. As a junior and a senior he became the star of the Laney varsity team, averaging more than 20 points a game.

No one was prouder of his achievements than his father. The two would maintain an extremely close relationship until James Jordan's death in 1993. Michael always described his father as his biggest fan. "I've got to believe one thing," James Jordan once said. "One day, God was sitting around and decided to make Himself the perfect basketball player. He gave him a little hardship early in life to make him appreciate what he would earn in the end, and called him Michael Jordan."

*When Jordan enrolled at the University of North Carolina, not many people knew who he was, but his coach quickly discovered that "we didn't have anybody who could guard him."*

# 3

# On Dean's List

Despite his success at Laney High School, Jordan was not regarded as a prize recruit by those colleges with the best basketball programs. As a senior, Jordan failed to make a list of the 300 top high school basketball players in the country.

But while other colleges were overlooking Jordan, Coach Dean Smith of the University of North Carolina (UNC) had been tipped off about him by assistant coach Roy Williams, who had seen Jordan play at a basketball camp. Wanting to see how Jordan would do against topflight competition, Williams arranged for Jordan to be invited to the famous Five Star basketball camp in Pittsburgh, Pennsylvania.

At Five Star, Jordan excelled against some of the top competition in the country. The player no one seemed to know about could not be stopped by anyone at the camp, no matter how much bigger they were in size or reputation. Jordan either went around or jumped over anyone who tried to guard him, and he was voted the MVP for both sessions he attended. Williams reported back to Smith that Jordan was a player UNC had to have. Jordan was just as fortunate, for every year the UNC Tar Heels were one of the country's best college teams.

On the UNC campus in the fall of 1981, Jordan quickly made a name for himself. A fellow student, Ken Stewart, remembered noticing Jordan playing in a pick-up game behind his dormitory. "He came out doing 360s, alley-oops, slamming over people, and that was the first we had heard of him," Stewart recalled.

Still, Jordan later confessed that when he started at UNC, "I thought everybody was a superstar and I would be the low man."

Those doubts did not last long. In his first week of practice, Coach Smith learned that "we didn't have anyone who could guard him." Soon afterward, Jordan was named a starter, a rare accomplishment for a freshman. After the first game, in which he scored 22 points, "I realized I was as good as everybody else," he said.

He only seemed to get better after that. "I've never seen anybody pick up the game so fast," his teammate James Worthy said. "Michael just doesn't make mistakes." At the end of the season, the coaches in the Atlantic Coast Conference (ACC), where Jordan played, voted him the league's freshman player of the year.

With Jordan adding his talents to an already excellent team, UNC easily won the ACC regular-season title and postseason tournament championship. Then it was on to the NCAA tournament.

The winner of this tournament is regarded as the country's national college-basketball champion.

Despite his success at UNC, Coach Smith had never won the NCAA championship. But in the spring of 1982, the talented Tar Heels moved easily through the tournament's opening rounds to the championship game at the Superdome in New Orleans. There, they were matched up against Georgetown University, who were led by a star freshman of their own, center Patrick Ewing.

The championship game was an extremely hard-fought contest right from the opening tip-off. With 32 seconds remaining, North Carolina, trail-

*Freshman Michael Jordan launches the shot that will give UNC coach Dean Smith his first NCAA championship.*

ing by 1 point, called for a time-out. The obvious play was to work the ball inside to Sam Perkins, the team's center, or to James Worthy, who had already burned the tough Georgetown defense for 28 points. But Smith knew that Georgetown would be ready for such a strategy. Instead, he decided to put the biggest game of his career as a coach in Jordan's hands. The final play was designed for Jordan to take the last shot.

With the game's last few seconds ticking away, Jordan received a pass on the left wing. He caught the ball and went up in the same motion. His jump shot at this stage in his career tended to be flat, without much arc. This time, though, he unleashed what he later described as "a rainbow."

In the stands of the Superdome, James Jordan covered his face with his hands as his son released the shot. Next to him, Deloris Jordan screamed in delight as the ball swished through the net, giving Carolina the lead. Seconds later, the clock ran out, and UNC was the national champion.

*Despite winning a national championship in his first year of college basketball, Jordan worked hard during the off-season and returned an even better player, particularly on defense.*

# 4

# The Most Awesome Player

When Jordan returned as a sophomore, Coach Smith was amazed to find that he had improved in every part of his game. For the past six months, Jordan had spent every spare moment practicing. The difference in his game, Smith said, "was like night and day."

An even better Jordan was a frightening thought for opponents, but the Tar Heels had not improved. Without Worthy, who had gone to the NBA, UNC was just not as good a team. Though the Tar Heels tied for the ACC regular-season title, they lost in the early rounds of both the conference and NCAA tournaments.

But Jordan's play received nothing but praise. In just his second year at the college level, Jordan was already being referred to by local reporters as the "best all around player in college basketball" and the "most talented player North Carolina or the ACC has ever seen." He was named national college player of the year by the *Sporting News,* and scouts predicted a brilliant professional career for him.

UNC thus approached its 1983–84 season with high hopes. The Tar Heels swept through the regular season with only one loss. Playing the best ball of his career, Jordan led the ACC in scoring at almost 20 points per game. For most of the season, UNC was ranked the number-one team in the country.

But once again, the Tar Heels had a rough *postseason.* They lost to inferior teams in the

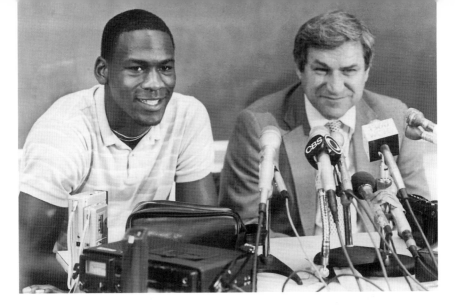

*Though Jordan's mother did not approve, Dean Smith (right) supported Jordan's decision to leave college before his senior year—hardly a rash act, considering* Sports Illustrated *had already called Jordan "merely the finest all-around amateur player in the world."*

semifinals of the ACC tournament and in the regional semifinals of the NCAA tournament.

The tournament losses marked a bitter end to Jordan's college career. Having again won several college player-of-the-year awards, he announced on May 5, 1984, that he would pass up his senior year at UNC to become a professional player.

But before turning pro, Jordan tried out for the basketball team that would represent the United States at the 1984 Summer Olympic Games. Because Jordan's incredible talent allowed him to achieve success using *unorthodox* methods, some people predicted that he would not get along with Bobby Knight, the team's coach. Knight believed in playing basketball the old-fashioned way, the fundamental way, and he could be very hard on players who did not follow his orders. A free-wheeling, flamboyant player like Jordan was not the kind of hoopster that Knight was comfortable coaching.

But to the surprise of many people, Knight realized that insisting that Jordan do things his way would stifle the young player's creativity. Instead, he recognized Jordan's extraordinary talent and allowed him the freedom he needed on the court. With Jordan leading the way, the U.S. team swept its way to the gold medal, winning every game by an average margin of 32 points.

Jordan was the third player taken in the 1984 NBA draft. (During a draft, professional teams take turns selecting players entering the league from college.) It took his new team, the Chicago Bulls, just a few practice games in training camp to recognize how good a player he truly was. No matter how the Chicago coach, Kevin Loughery, divided up his players for practice games, one thing remained the same: the team that had Jordan always won.

The rest of the league soon learned the same thing. Usually one of the league's worst teams,

*Jordan celebrates the U.S. team's gold medal in the Pan-American Games in 1983. The following year saw Jordan and the United States win another gold medal at the Olympics.*

Chicago now found itself performing in sold-out arenas as word spread about Jordan's spectacular play. He quickly became the league's most popular player and biggest box office draw. His television commercials for his sneakers, Air Jordans, helped make the shoe's manufacturer, Nike, the most successful company of its kind in the world. Young basketball players around the country began wearing very long, very baggy shorts on the basketball court, just like the ones Michael wore.

After playing against Jordan just once, Larry Bird of the Boston Celtics, whom many considered the league's top player, said that the Chicago rookie was the best player ever. Even so, Jordan could not make the Bulls a great team by himself. Although he led his team in scoring, rebounding, and *assists*, which was something that only two other players in history had ever done, the Bulls won just 38 of their 82 games. They were easily eliminated in the first round of the playoffs.

Jordan easily won the Rookie of the Year award, but his personal success did not make him

*Jordan's explosive rookie season left opponents awestruck and inspired $130 million in sales of a brand-new basketball shoe, Air Jordans.*

happy. Losing frustrated him, and he believed that several of his teammates were not as dedicated to the game as they should have been.

The 1985–86 season was even more disappointing for him. The Bulls were no better, even though they had fired Coach Loughery. To make matters worse, in the third game of the season, Jordan broke a small bone in his left foot while running upcourt. As a high school, college, or professional player, Jordan had never missed a game, but now he had to sit out 63 of them while his foot healed.

Against his doctor's advice, Jordan returned to the court on March 15, 1986, near the end of the regular season. His return allowed the Bulls to sneak into the playoffs and set the stage for one of the most incredible performances in NBA history. In the second game of the opening round of the playoffs, while playing against the eventual NBA champions, the Boston Celtics, Jordan scored an astounding 63 points. Again and again, he went over and around a host of bewildered Boston defenders.

In the game's most memorable moment, Jordan found himself pinned with the ball in the right corner by Bird. Juking in several different directions while dribbling the ball rapidly back and forth between his legs, Jordan created an illusion of motion that sent Bird scurrying backward. He then zigzagged by three Boston players along the baseline before sailing under the hoop to its far side, where he dropped a twisting *reverse layup* off the backboard.

Though Chicago lost the series in three straight games, Jordan had again impressed Bird. "I think he's God disguised as Michael Jordan," Bird said afterward. "He is the most awesome player in the NBA."

*Jordan's soaring acrobatics left many half-convinced that he could fly. The breathtaking beauty of his gravity-defying dunks arguably outstripped even the aerial artistry of the legendary Julius Erving.*

# 5

# The Jordan Rules

Over the next several seasons, Jordan would rise to even greater heights. Unfortunately, his teammates were almost never able to lift their own games to his level.

Jordan followed up his performance in the 1986 playoffs with a one-man assault on the record books that lasted the course of the entire next season. When he was through, he had won the first of seven consecutive scoring titles, scoring at a higher rate than any guard in NBA history—an astounding 37.1 points per game.

The season was a *cavalcade* of personal highlights. Jordan scored 50 or more points in a game nine separate times. He scored 61 points in a game twice. During one streak, he scored 40 or more points in nine consecutive contests. In the season opener, he scored 50 points against the New York Knicks. Three weeks later, against the same opponent, he scored his team's final 18 points, including the game-winning jump shot with eight seconds left to play. Later in the season, he set an NBA record by scoring 23 consecutive points against the Atlanta Hawks.

In addition to his scoring feats, Jordan became the first player in NBA history to record more than 100 blocked shots and 200 steals in the same season. He received more votes than any other player for the All-Star game, and he won the annual midseason slam dunk contest. His popularity with fans grew even greater, and he became the most admired athlete in America. To make matters complete, he met Juanita Vanoy, a bank officer, who would become his wife and the mother of their three children.

But for Jordan there was still disappointment, for the Bulls were still not a very good team. In 1986–87, they won just 40 of their 82 games and were again eliminated in the first round of the playoffs.

To basketball experts, Jordan was definitely the game's most spectacular player. Still, most of them regarded either Larry Bird or Magic Johnson of the Los Angeles Lakers as the best all-around player in the game. The reason was simple: Bird's Celtics and Johnson's Lakers won NBA championships. In Bird's years with the team, the Celtics had won three championships and lost in the finals two other times. Before Magic's playing career was over, the Lakers would win five championships and make nine trips to the NBA finals.

Though both Bird and Johnson were great scorers, they were best known for their passing. Critics said that Bird and Johnson made their teammates better, while Jordan's one-on-one style of play rewarded only himself. Many people also pointed out that no player had ever led the league in scoring and played on a championship team in the same season.

Such criticism angered Jordan. Before the 1987–88 season began, he gave an interview in which he said that Johnson and Bird both had much better teammates to play with than he did. Most of the other Celtics and Lakers starting players were also All-Stars, Jordan pointed out, but no one else on the Bulls was. The statement annoyed Jordan's teammates, but it was undeniably true. For the next several years, Jordan would constantly demand that the management of the Bulls get better players for the team.

In many ways, Jordan's 1987–88 season was even better than the record-breaking one of the year before. His scoring average declined two points to 35 points per game, but his shooting percentage rose from a fine 48 percent to a superb 54 percent. His rebounds and assists totals also increased. He was clearly an even steadier, more well-rounded player, and he was voted the NBA's most valuable player for the first time. Amazingly, he was also honored as the league's best defensive player. He is the only player in history to win an MVP, a scoring championship, and a Defensive Player of the Year award in the same season.

Even better, as far as Jordan was concerned, was that the Bulls were becoming a stronger team. Rookies Horace Grant and Scottie Pippen and forward Charles Oakley gave Jordan the help he needed. The Bulls won 50 games, and for the first time in Jordan's career they advanced past the first round of the playoffs. With Jordan averaging a *phenomenal* 45 points per game, the Bulls defeated the Cleveland Cavaliers.

But then Chicago ran into the Detroit Pistons. The Pistons had become the Bulls' most hated rival. The bad blood between the two teams went back a long way. Detroit's best player, the wonderful *point guard* Isiah Thomas, was jealous of Jordan's success and popularity. Jordan himself

*The arrival of Scottie Pippen, shown here sailing in for a luscious finger-roll against the Houston Rockets, was a key turning point in the Bulls' gradual transformation into a championship contender.*

did not like Thomas, who reportedly had once convinced Jordan's teammates in the All-Star Game not to pass him the ball.

More important, by that time Detroit had become one of the league's best teams—a team the

Bulls had to learn how to beat if Jordan was ever to match Bird and Johnson in championships. The secret of the Pistons' success was an extremely physical style of defensive play. Jordan, his teammates, and many other players in the league felt that the Pistons consistently and intentionally crossed the fine line that separates physical and aggressive basketball from dirty and dangerous play.

The Pistons clutched and grabbed, they held, they elbowed, and they undercut. When they *fouled,* they fouled hard, trying to intimidate opponents or at least sap their determination. Their aim was to slow the pace of each game to a virtual crawl, turning each contest into the NBA equivalent of a street fight. Jordan felt that Detroit players had intentionally tried to injure him several times.

Such a style was especially frustrating to the Bulls. With Jordan and Pippen, Chicago relied on *finesse* rather than brute force, and the Bulls played best when the pace of the game was quick.

For three years running, from 1987–88 through 1989–90, the Pistons dominated the Bulls, finishing ahead of them in the Central Division each year and then defeating them in the playoffs.

In addition to their physical style, the Pistons dominated the Bulls with a strategy known as The Jordan Rules. The Jordan Rules were a set of defensive principles that were designed to keep the best scorer the game had ever known in check. Essentially, they were very simple. All five Detroit players had to be aware of where Jordan was at all times. He was to be *double-teamed* every time he touched the ball. There was an unspoken Jordan rule as well: Knock him down every time he drove to the basket.

The Jordan Rules consistently frustrated the Chicago star and his teammates. Although Jordan still scored against Detroit at a high rate, the Pistons made him work extremely hard for his points. Forced to score much more than they usually had to, Jordan's teammates usually wilted under Detroit's defensive pressure and physical intimidation.

Almost single-handedly, Jordan was still able to extend the Pistons to a seventh game in

*Jordan is unceremoniously trampled by Isiah Thomas and Joe Dumars of the Detroit Pistons during the 1990 playoffs. Despite the marked improvement of the Chicago Bulls in the late 1980s, they were frustrated time and again in the playoffs by the rough, tough Pistons.*

both the 1989 and 1990 playoffs. But in both of those years his teammates failed to give him the support he needed, and the Bulls went down to defeat in the crucial contest. Meanwhile, Detroit went on to claim the NBA championship that Jordan so desperately wanted for himself and his team.

For Jordan, the worst defeat took place in the spring of 1990. Chicago's 55 wins that year had given it the second-best regular-season record in the league. Even though the best record belonged to the hated Pistons, the Bulls and their fans were confident that this would be the year Chicago would eliminate Detroit in the playoffs and move on to the championship round.

Jordan had put in his usual brilliant regular season, leading the league in scoring for the fourth consecutive year, making the All-NBA first team for the fourth of seven consecutive years, making the NBA All-Defense first team for the third of six consecutive years, and playing what he would describe as his "greatest game," a performance against the Cleveland Cavaliers in which he tallied 69 points and 18 rebounds.

Jordan had then prepared for the showdown with Detroit by playing what he described as the best four consecutive games of his life. In the course of Chicago's five-game playoff series win over the Philadelphia 76ers, he had averaged 43 points, 7 rebounds, and 7 assists.

His teammates also seemed better prepared for Detroit. Center Bill Cartwright had arrived in a trade for Oakley, giving the Bulls the proven *low-post* scorer they had always lacked in Jordan's time with the club. After three years in the league, Pippen was becoming a remarkable player, a Jordanesque combination of height, quickness, speed, explosive leaping ability, and offensive creativity. Chicago also featured a new head coach: Laid-back but demanding Phil Jackson had replaced hard-driving Doug Collins. Most of the players greatly preferred Jackson's approach.

But after two games against Detroit, there seemed little reason for Chicago to be hopeful. The

*The Bulls' improvement did not come fast enough for the intensely competitive Jordan. Though they won 55 games in the 1989–90 season and pushed the league-champion Pistons to the limit in the playoffs, Jordan's teammates once again crumpled in the deciding seventh game.*

Pistons won both games easily, holding the Bulls to sickly totals of 77 and 93 points. Jordan, meanwhile, averaged just 27 points per game, five below his average, and shot less than 40 percent shooting. As always against Detroit, his teammates appeared unsure of themselves. Jordan's partners in the backcourt, Craig Hodges and John Paxson, missed all their shots in game one. Pippen admitted to being intimidated by the defense of Dennis Rodman.

Then Chicago regrouped. Jordan averaged more than 40 points a game as the Bulls won three of the next four contests, setting up a deciding game seven. But though Jordan scored or assisted on every Chicago basket of the second half until he left the game, Detroit won easily, 93–74. As had happened in previous years against Detroit, Jordan's teammates "disappeared" at critical moments. Pippen shot just 1 for 10 from the floor. Grant shot 3 for 17. B. J. Armstrong was 1 for 8, and Craig Hodges was 3 for 13.

For the series, Jordan shot 47 percent from the floor. This was below average for him, but it was exceptional against Detroit's superb defense. Meanwhile, his teammates managed only an atrocious 38 percent. "We have to do some things. We have to make some changes," a grim Jordan said in the sad Chicago locker room after the last game.

*When Bulls coach Phil Jackson (left) installed a new system, Jordan had a lot of doubts at first. But Jackson's strategy turned out to be just what the Bulls needed to raise their play to championship level.*

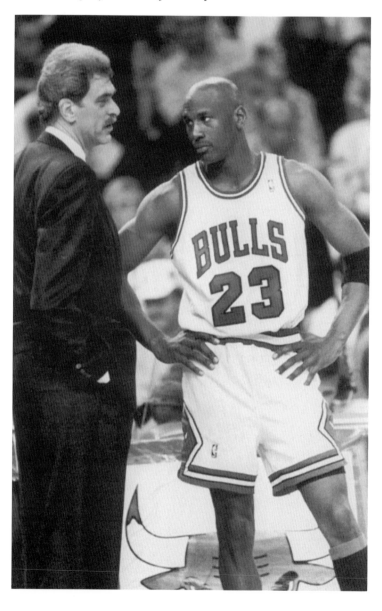

# 6
# Those Championship Seasons

To Jordan's great anger, the Bulls did not make any major trades prior to the beginning of the 1990–91 season. Jordan believed that this left Chicago again unprepared to contend for a championship. Disappointed, he began to talk about retiring. He was tired, he said, of being so famous that he could not even go out to eat without drawing a crowd. He had even begun to find that basketball was something of a chore. The game, he said, was now more "like a business."

The season did not begin well for the Bulls. Jordan did not like Coach Jackson's new offensive system, which called on the other Bulls to take more shots. He warned that if the new strategy did not work, he was going to have to shoot more himself. He also got mad when the Chicago management ignored his suggestions for trades. Jordan said the Chicago team was simply not good enough to win the championship.

Jordan had said such things in the past, and he had been right. Now things were different. Chicago did not need new players, because the ones they had were getting better. Even more important, the Bulls were learning how to play together as a team, which is the hardest thing for any group of basketball players to learn.

For example, at first Jordan had not thought that Bill Cartwright was a good player. Jordan thought that the Bulls center was clumsy, but Cartwright proved that he could be a very good scorer and effective defender. The youngest starters for the Bulls, Pippen and Grant, were improving with each year they played in the NBA. They had now reached the point where they could be considered All-Stars. In John Paxson, a deadly outside shooter, Chicago found the perfect partner for Jordan in the backcourt.

Coach Jackson also made a huge difference. He realized that Jordan's tremendous defensive skills could be as big a weapon as his ability to score. Pippen and Grant were excellent defensive players also. All three of them were quick enough and big enough to guard virtually any player. This allowed Chicago to double-team and press other teams in the backcourt. Assistant Coach John Bach called the three "the Dobermans," and Jackson unleashed them. Soon, Chicago was devastating opponents with a series of traps and presses that led to turnovers, fast breaks, and easy baskets.

The easy baskets led to even easier wins. Soon, Chicago became a team that was as feared for its defense as was Detroit. As the Bulls got better, Jordan supported and encouraged his teammates more. He and Pippen became especially friendly, and Pippen soon became the league's second-best player. This gave Chicago a two-pronged attack that no team in the league could match.

With Jordan winning his fifth-straight scoring title and second MVP award, the Bulls swept through the regular season, winning 61 games to finish on top of the Central Division. They then steamrolled through the first two rounds of the playoffs, losing only one game on their way to the conference finals and a fourth straight postseason *rendezvous* with the Pistons.

For the Bulls, the series turned out to be surprisingly easy. Chicago defeated Detroit in four straight games, dominating every contest. They even imitated the Pistons' bullying approach. "They stole our playbook," said Detroit forward John Salley afterward. "Talking junk, talking garbage, making sure there is only one shot, keeping people out of the middle, making people beat them with their jump shot. That's what we usually do."

Chicago's victory set up a dream matchup in the NBA finals with the Los Angeles Lakers. In Magic Johnson's twelfth year with the club, the Lakers were making a remarkable ninth appearance in the championship round. But the showdown again proved to be a mismatch. After losing the opening game on a last-second shot, the Bulls handily won four straight contests to claim the NBA crown. With Magic handcuffed by Pippen's remarkable defense, Jordan dominated every phase of the game. He even had more assists than Johnson, who was generally regarded as the greatest passer in the NBA.

There now seemed to be no doubt about who was the best all-around player in basketball. In the happy Chicago locker room after the final game of the series, Jordan wept tears of joy and hugged the gold championship trophy as if he would never let it go.

In the 1991–92 season, Chicago romped through the regular season with an absolutely incredible total of 67 wins. Jordan won his sixth straight scoring championship and second straight MVP award. In the playoffs, Chicago whipped the Miami Heat, New York Knicks, and Cleveland Cavaliers and returned to the finals for the second straight year.

Their opponents this time were the Portland Trailblazers, who were led by *shooting guard* Clyde Drexler. Some sportswriters had made the mistake of suggesting that Drexler was Jordan's equal as an all-around player. It took Jordan just the first half of the first game of the championship series to end that talk. In the first 24 minutes of the series, Jordan scorched Drexler for six three-point *field goals* on the way to 35 points. Both totals were playoff records for a half.

Drexler never recovered. He spent the rest of the series chasing after Jordan and taking bad shots, and his team actually played better when he was on the bench. Chicago won its second straight title in six games. That summer, Jordan displayed his dominance again, this time as the brightest of the NBA stars who made up the U.S. Dream Team that won the gold medal in basketball at the Summer Olympic Games in Barcelona, Spain.

Once again, Jordan considered retiring. There seemed to be nothing else for him to prove on the basketball court. His father thought that he should quit, but Jordan decided that there was still one more goal for him to reach. He wanted to accomplish something that neither Larry Bird nor

*Flanked by teammates Scottie Pippen and Clyde Drexler, Jordan celebrates a victory by the U.S. "Dream Team," which took the gold medal at the 1992 Olympics.*

Magic Johnson had been able to achieve. He wanted to win a third *straight* NBA championship.

In the 1992–93 season, Jordan casually claimed his record-tying seventh straight scoring crown. The Bulls posted only the league's third-best regular-season record, but they regrouped in the playoffs. With Jordan playing at a *phenomenal* level, even for him, they rallied past the New York Knicks to advance to the NBA finals against the Phoenix Suns.

The Suns were led by forward Charles Barkley, a remarkable player and close friend of Jordan's who had won the MVP award for his fine play in the regular season. But in the championship round, Jordan again demonstrated that there could be no doubt that he was the league's best player. He averaged an *unprecedented* 41 points per game, another record for the championship round, and led Chicago to a six-game victory. The Bulls became the first NBA team to win three straight championships in almost 30 years.

After the season ended, sportswriters and fans debated whether the Bulls could now be considered one of the greatest teams ever.

Almost no one, however, disputed whether Jordan could now be called the greatest player of all time. He had answered that question beyond argument on the basketball court.

Jordan himself seemed to feel that there were no more challenges left for him on the basketball floor. Just several days before the Bulls were to begin training camp in October 1993, he announced his retirement from the game. Although his beloved father had been murdered that past summer, Jordan said that the death had little to do with his decision. No, his reasons for leaving were much simpler than that. There were no more challenges for him on the court, and he had always planned to go out on top. He had, he said, nothing left to prove.

Instead, he set out to prove himself in a different sport. Jordan and his father had often

*Michael and his father, James Jordan (right), were very close. When James Jordan was murdered in 1993, Michael was devastated.*

talked about his boyhood dream of becoming a professional baseball player. Now, with his father gone, he decided to make that dream a reality.

At the age of 32, Jordan became a minor league baseball player with the Birmingham Barons, a Double-A farm team of the Chicago White Sox. His goal, he said, was to someday make it to the major leagues as an outfielder.

Wherever the Barons played in the summer of 1994, the stands were packed. The fans came to see the curious spectacle of the world's most famous athlete starting from scratch at a new sport. But like basketball players, baseball players only make it to the top after years of hard work and practice at their game.

Jordan was a tremendous athlete, but since high school he had concentrated only on basketball. It was too much to expect that at the age of 32 he could make up for all the years of playing baseball that he had missed. Some people believe that hitting a baseball is the hardest task in sports. Whether that is true or not, Michael Jordan certainly found it harder than sinking a basket. As a Baron, he was a very weak hitter, batting just .202 and hitting only 3 home runs. He showed his greatest potential as a baseball player on the base paths, where he stole 30 bases.

By the spring of 1995, Jordan was willing to give up on his baseball experiment. The NBA regular season was winding down, and the

*At the age of 32, Jordan decided to pursue his dream of becoming a professional baseball player. His late start was too much to overcome, however, and when baseball was crippled by a strike in the spring of 1995, he bolted back to the NBA.*

playoffs were approaching. He was starting to feel the old desire, the hunger to go out and prove himself once more to be the best basketball player in the world.

Before Jordan's retirement, a fourth NBA title would have added little to his legend. But now, the challenge facing Jordan was much more difficult. Though less than two years had passed since his departure, the Bulls were not the same championship squad he had left behind. Their starting center, Bill Cartwright, had gone to the

Seattle Supersonics, and their All-Star power for-ward, Horace Grant, had signed as a free agent with the up-and-coming Orlando Magic. Even with the world's best shooting guard lighting up the scoreboard, it would be tough to overcome the loss of their two best big men. Without their *rebounding,* scoring, and defense in the middle, the Bulls would seemingly be at the mercy of teams with dominating centers such as Shaquille O'Neal, Patrick Ewing, Hakeem Olajuwon, and David Robinson. The task facing Jordan was so *daunting* that many considered it impossible. Two years before, there had been nothing left for him to prove in the NBA, but now he had a new mountain to climb, and he was happy.

There were many new challenges ahead for Jordan. Could he return from retirement and prove himself to be as great a player as he once was? Could he outshine the NBA's newest stars, such as Shaquille O'Neal and Anfernee Hardaway of the Orlando Magic, the team that many people expected would take Chicago's place as the best in

*After he had won everything there was to win and proved everything there was to prove in the NBA, professional basketball was no longer fun for Jordan. But coming back from retirement offered him the challenge he needed to light his competitive fires again.*

the league? Could he become the first player in the history of the NBA to come back from retirement and lead his team to a league championship? With the very simplest of announcements—"I'm back"—he set out to answer all those questions.

# Career Statistics

**MICHAEL JEFFREY JORDAN**
(Chicago Bulls)

| YEAR | G | MIN | FGM | FGA | PCT | FTM | FTA | PCT | RBD | AST | PTS | AVG |
|---|---|---|---|---|---|---|---|---|---|---|---|---|
| 1984-85 | 82 | 3,144 | 837 | 1,625 | .515 | 630 | 746 | .845 | 534 | 481 | 2,313 | 28.2 |
| 1985-86 | 18 | 451 | 150 | 328 | .457 | 105 | 125 | .840 | 64 | 53 | 408 | 22.7 |
| 1986-87 | 82 | 3,281 | 1,098 | 2,279 | .482 | 833 | 972 | .857 | 430 | 377 | 3,041 | 37.1 |
| 1987-88 | 82 | 3,311 | 1,069 | 1,998 | .535 | 723 | 860 | .841 | 449 | 485 | 2,868 | 35.0 |
| 1988-89 | 81 | 3,255 | 966 | 1,795 | .538 | 674 | 793 | .850 | 652 | 650 | 2,633 | 32.5 |
| 1989-90 | 82 | 3,197 | 1,034 | 1,964 | .526 | 593 | 699 | .848 | 565 | 519 | 2,753 | 33.6 |
| 1990-91 | 82 | 3,034 | 990 | 1,837 | .539 | 571 | 671 | .851 | 492 | 453 | 2,580 | 31.5 |
| 1991-92 | 80 | 3,102 | 943 | 1,818 | .519 | 491 | 590 | .832 | 511 | 489 | 2,404 | 30.1 |
| 1992-93 | 78 | 3,067 | 992 | 2,003 | .495 | 476 | 569 | .837 | 522 | 428 | 2,541 | 32.6 |
| 1994-95 | 17 | 668 | 166 | 404 | .411 | 109 | 136 | .801 | 117 | 90 | 457 | 26.9 |
| Totals | 684 | 26,510 | 8,245 | 16,051 | .514 | 5,205 | 6,161 | .845 | 4,336 | 4,025 | 21,998 | 31.0 |
| Playoff Totals | 121 | 5,065 | 1,531 | 3,066 | .499 | 1,006 | 1,208 | .833 | 806 | 783 | 4,165 | 34.4 |

| | |
|---|---|
| G | games |
| MIN | minutes |
| FGA | field goals attempted |
| FGM | field goals made |
| PCT | percent |
| FTA | free throws attempted |
| FTM | free throws made |
| RBD | rebounds |
| AST | assists |
| PTS | points |
| AVG | scoring average |

# Further Reading

Dolan, Sean. *Magic Johnson.* New York: Chelsea House, 1993.

Naughton, Jim. *Taking to the Air.* New York: Warner, 1992.

Sakamoo, Bob. *Michael "Air" Jordan—MVP and NBA Champ.* Lincolnwood, IL: Publications International, 1991.

Smith, Sam. *The Jordan Rules: The Inside Story of a Turbulent Season with Michael Jordan and the Chicago Bulls.* New York: Simon & Schuster, 1992.

Stauth, Cameron. *The Golden Boys: The Unauthorized Inside Look at the U.S. Olympic Basketball Team.* New York: Simon & Schuster, 1992.

# Glossary

**assists**    passes leading to points scored by a teammate

**cavalcade**    a series of things following one after the other

**daunting**    frightening or difficult to face

**field goals**    baskets other than free throws

**finesse**    clever, skillful, or quick movements or behavior

**double-teamed**    guarded by two players

**foul**    contact between players that breaks the rules of basketball

**foul shots**    free shots awarded to a player who is fouled; also known as free throws

**fourth quarter**    the final period of a basketball game

**low-post**    near the basket; low-post players (the center and the power forward) need great height and strength

**phenomenal**    incredible; amazing

**point guard**    the position responsible for passing and directing the team's offense.

**postseason**   playoff tournament games following the regular season that determine conference and league championships

**rebounding**   grabbing a loose ball after a missed shot

**rendezvous**   a meeting (from the French word pronounced RON-day-voo)

**reverse layup**   a basket scored by leaping toward the rim, flying past it, and flipping the ball in from the far side

**rookie**   a first-year player

**shell-shocked**   stunned and frightened, as from an explosion

**shooting guard**   the position usually played by a team's best shooter and scorer

**tip-off**   the start of a basketball game, when a ball is tossed between two players who try to tip it to a teammate; also called a jump ball

**unorthodox**   different from the normal way of doing things

**unprecedented**   never having happened before

**vanquished**   beaten; defeated

# Chronology

| | |
|---|---|
| **1963** | Michael Jeffrey Jordan born on February 17 in Brooklyn, New York |
| **1982** | Scores winning points that give University of North Carolina the national collegiate championship |
| **1984** | Drafted by the Chicago Bulls; sparks U.S. team to gold medal in Olympics |
| **1985** | Wins NBA Rookie of the Year Award |
| **1986** | Breaks a bone in his foot; sets playoff scoring records against the Boston Celtics |
| **1987** | Wins first of seven consecutive scoring championships |
| **1991** | Chicago wins the NBA championship |
| **1992** | Wins third MVP award and second Olympic gold medal; Chicago wins second straight NBA championship |
| **1993** | Named to NBA all-defensive team for sixth straight season; Chicago wins third straight NBA title; Jordan retires from the NBA |
| **1994** | Becomes a professional baseball player |
| **1995** | Abandons baseball and rejoins the NBA |

# Index

**Sean Dolan** has a degree in literature and American history from SUNY Oswego. He is the author of many biographies and histories for young adult readers, including *James Beckwourth* and *Magic Johnson* in the BLACK AMERICANS OF ACHIEVEMENT series, and has edited a series of volumes on the famous explorers of history.

## PICTURE CREDITS